God Doesn't Live at Our House Anymore

poems by

Charlotte Clear

Finishing Line Press
Georgetown, Kentucky

God Doesn't Live at Our House Anymore

ACKNOWLEDGMENTS

I am the mother of three children. My son, Jake, and my younger son Alex. My daughter, Charlotte, would have turned fifteen on January 3, 2023. She died for no medical reason. This was the watershed event in my life as a person, as a writer, and as a parent.

It is always painful to look at one's failures, but none more so than those as a mother. In Spanish we say, "Me da verguenza." It gives me shame.

I did not drive my sons to soccer. I did not join the PTA. I did not make cookies for the bake sale at school; I did not sell gift wrap or magazine subscriptions for their elementary school fundraisers. I did not check their homework. This was not so much negligence as absence. Although we all lived under the same roof I was traveling elsewhere, to the land of grief. I was eighteen years sober when my daughter died. I suffered a nervous breakdown and a relapse after 18 years of sobriety when Charlotte died. Shortly after her death, from this place of abject despair, I returned to writing multiple genres: creative nonfiction, fiction and poetry.

I missed two years of my sons' childhood following the death of my daughter and this guilt and failure is a theme in my second chapbook, *God Doesn't Live At Our House Anymore*, where I address my daughter's inexplicable death and the impact it had on my entire family, particularly on my sons and myself. *God Doesn't Live at Our House Anymore* is a collection of poems that directly relates to my life as a mother before my daughter died and afterwards.

My family life both inspires and challenges my artistic career; I am caught between the urgency of writing for its own therapeutic process and the ongoing needs of my children, writing became a creative medium to return to a spiritual and emotional sense of wellness.

Publisher: Leah Huete de Maines
Editor: Christen Kincaid
Cover Art: *Frozen Charlotte* by Anne Carney, https://www.facebook.com/worksbyanne
Author Photo: Andy Cohen
Cover Design: Elizabeth Maines McCleavy

Order online: www.finishinglinepress.com
also available on amazon.com

Author inquiries and mail orders:
Finishing Line Press
PO Box 1626
Georgetown, Kentucky 40324
USA

Contents

For Allan

I.
"That's why we labor to bring love into this world"

II.
"The Baby died—we had nothing"

—William Kotswinkle, *Summer in the Secret Sea*

Infidelity

I
My long, lithe legs
lifted upon your broad Aryan shoulders,
spread as wide as the gulf
that accompanies us on our honeymoon in Bali
follows us across many oceans, many times zones
settles in our marriage
landing on Riverside Drive and 112th Street,
where we see the shores of the Harlem River
from our roof top garden where the
purple Mandeville and white Hibiscus I plant
die on their vines from neglect or drought or futility.
much like romance.

II
We lay in the airless loft bed
of our one-bedroom apartment
the size of an overseas postage stamp
on a postcard we mailed overseas
and never thought about again
until it returns to us.
Only then do we remember to worry.

III
I say to my husband, *"It's that time of month."*
His graceful Swiss hands rest behind his head
as if he searched for stars on the ceiling we could touch.

"We have to try,"
as if sex were a household chore or a task on a to do list—
like pay the mortgage,
take out the recycling,
separate glass from paper.
pick up the dry cleaning
load the dishwasher, check the mail,
find the super to fix leaky faucets
replace dead light bulbs.

I commute to work,
cross an errand off
my to-do list that grows
longer every day.

My husband says nothing which tells me everything.

Indentured Servitude

I.

I eat anger for dinner.
I imagine the promised land: Divorce
after wandering forty years in the desert,
desperate for a drink.

My sacrifices age me, make me bitter.
I mourn the monotonous years endured
only to arrive at this place of
exile.

II.

I dread coming home to this lonely, loveless house.
dream of old lovers, a man who once kissed me there.
I somehow don't do enough or perform tasks well.
My children wither me.
I do not bloom again in the spring.
I produce offspring I no longer recognize
or even like anymore.
I lose my sense of humor
under the weight of so many unbearable obligations.

I lie to other parents at the playground,
even to myself, the truth, unbearable.
We all lie.

III.

I eat standing up, longing for bedtime.
I learn to sleep with my eyes open.
When my husband moves to the living room.
I don't notice.
When I finally realize he is gone, I don't miss him.
I lock myself in the bathroom to be alone and lonely.

The dinner dishes still are in the sink.
They will be there tomorrow.
Like my husband, like my son, my claustrophobia and my exhaustion.

My son cries. I put the newspaper down.
I look at my fat, middle aged husband who has fallen asleep on the couch.

IV.
It is 8:00 at night.
The second shift begins.
I rise, stifling my anger and frustration as it devours me.
I go to my insatiable son. I hold his hand.
I nurse him in my marital bed, too tired to travel to his nursery
with its pastel animal mobile, Pottery Barn crib sheets, airplane rug,
Aunt Rachel's baby present needlepoint of animals and letters.
Portending great happiness.
I wait for him to fall asleep. I breathe Jake's breath as if it were my own.
that familiar, that intimate.
I look at his small heart and his huge demands.
I endure motherhood, hoping for parole.

The Lottery

We are stoned in the village for adultery:
nothing noble about our middle-aged affair.
When we fuck, we rattle the cages of unhappy couples.

Playgrounds howl with outrage—
park benches expose us.
We sacrifice respectability,
rendered reckless by the redundancy
of purple dinosaurs, train tracks,
swimming lessons, diaper genies.
Hunchbacked by marriage counseling, anti-depressants:
futile attempts to salvage a dying marriage.

Our failure at our own marriages,
leads us to kiss under the George Washington Bridge.
Our wreckage propels us:
the daily assault of obligations
strips us of romance, forbids innocence.
The irrelevance of our spouses
irritate us. Brazen with disappointment,
We grow reckless for relief.

We arrive naked, expecting nothing.
rendered speechless by this dangerous touch.
There is no spontaneous mercy.
Only restraining orders, handcuffs
my blue Longchamps overnight bag
abandoned on Bennett Avenue
when she ran us off the street.

You beg me not to call your wife.

We Try Again

I.
We bring our litany of accusations
spread them out on a green felt card table.

Our cards restless.
We have quick wrists.
We hedge our bets, wager.
We wait for each other to fold.
We lost our winning hand,
our poker face, all of our chips spent, Bankrupt

II.
Casinos bar us for our sadness.
We gamble on the inevitability of our own bad habits.
We learn to live without each other.
We grow stronger from this hardship.
We sacrifice the Queen of Hearts and
Ace of Spades left with the Joker.

III.
Our injuries, the cruel words
we inflicted on one another
take an entire brutal decade
until they ultimately fade.
Still, we pick at them, like grievances,
expose fresh wounds, new addictions.
We remember the awful.
Forget what abandonment
brought us to the Roulette Table,
which reminds me of Stendhal's Le Rouge and Le Noir
Stendhal a lost lover—
a house of cards, a winning streak exhausted.
Neither one of us apologizes or
makes excuses.

IV.
A year passes. We take new lovers.
We are momentarily happy. Then, we are not.
We recognize each other in these other strangers.
We cannot tolerate the resemblance.
We take them hostage,
but when they inevitably make demands of us,
they lose their utility.
We discard these one night stands more quickly.

V.
You find yourself alone again.
It rains. You wonder where I am.
If I have Diamonds or Spades—
Hearts, Clubs. A full house or a losing hand.
We arrange to meet that summer.
the space between us—
has grown infinite and treacherous.

You travel as far south as land permits.

I move further east. Our history follows us everywhere.

The Unbearable

We awaken in February—already weary.
You dress me with hands that have been lovers for decades, not
stolen hours.
We speak Portuguese for comfort.
English words for miscarriage too literal,
too clinical, absent aching.
We eat but are not hungry.
You drive. The traffic is swollen and pregnant.
When we enter the city,
I begin to cry.

The doctor speaks to us only in verbs and nouns:
The mechanics of miscarriage—
how an emergency D and C is a valuable service
But I see no value in this unspeakable procedure.

The only sound in the room is the scraping of my uterus.
captured in a teaspoon of tears.
Your hands shield my eyes, the gift of darkness.
They mask your grief, my body, our loss,
shared but separate, like solitary confinement.
Our days now as joyless as a flat line on the EKG
at Columbia Presbyterian Hospital's
Maternity ward,
absent our baby. Absent joy.
We lick each other off.
You bathe me as though
I were frail and blind. And I am.

Judas

I.
"La carne es flaca," me dice ella.
"He was a handsome man, she continues,
but had false eyes."

The kitchen is quiet with the sound of children dreaming.
I stub out my cigarette, a violent gesture.
"Everything about the man was false."
On Mothers' day I gather your emails, your love letters
your photos of our trip to Cornwall
to scatter our daughters' ashes.

I travel alone to North Island to gather kindling,
forage for decaying branches. Symbolic.
Rotten, dead wood that smells of mold, the aroma of infinite errors.
I gather my memories of you and our daughter.
build a bonfire in the backyard. I exorcise your impact.
I need to erase the residue of bitter ash, embers of despair
when she dies. Abandoning me to you.

My true love says to me:
"Be comforted.
There is a special place in hell for that man."
I light a match underneath your righteousness, your Scottish lover and
your cowardice.

Before and After

I. Before

My daughter Charlotte is my sacrifice.
I lose everything for her.
By the time I reach Columbia Presbyterian Labor and Delivery Room,
she is dead. "No medical reason."
Residents place me on the fifth floor,
where unimaginable things happen,
far away from the maternity ward.

Savage noises escape from me.
If it is sound, it is unrecognizable—
only dogs can hear the howling pitch.

II.

In the morning orderlies in green pajamas
bring her upstairs from the morgue.
I visualize her ride in the elevator
in her steel bassinet and wonder
if she senses movement.
I open her diaper.
I need the confirmation that her body parts
were perfect, intact,
that all ten toes stretch towards me,
like her clenched fingers.

I try gently to pry them open but cannot.
The dead clench their fists to the living.

I feed her my milk.
It leaks down my hospital gown
mimics morphine tears.

III.

My secretary Tawanna says:
"If you want to dance naked in the street,
I will stop the traffic for you."
I will always remember that.
I take her words home from the hospital,
instead of my daughter.

Smoking Jesus holds Charlotte in her arms,
"She looks just like Alex," her brother.
This makes me cry harder,
frantically push the morphine drip,
more medication. More.
I cannot get enough pain medication
now that Charlotte has died.
No poppy fields can quench my mourner's suffering.

I. *After*

Trespass. Her funeral destroys my privacy.
Strangers attend, uninvited. People from New Jersey.
I know not how.

Why would I want them present, to witness this? *This.*

At the funeral home I set myself on fire.
I don't notice the smoke, the hole
in my Barney's black cashmere dress.
I stop noticing things.
I walk into oncoming traffic.
A friend pulls me back to the curb,
but I don't feel any safer.
In fact, I never feel safe again after Charlotte dies.

II.

Condolence Cards arrive.
I don't open them.
I don't write thank you notes.
I don't answer the phone anymore or return calls.
I shut the ringer off the phone.
There is nobody I want to speak to,
except Charlotte.
She should be fifteen this January.
Still, I don't turn the ringer back on.

What She Wore

I
They don't let mothers
Into the morgue
to dress their dead daughters.
So, I do not remember
what Charlotte wore
when they transported her to the crematorium.
Maybe the pathologist,
ambulance driver,
hospital attendant
In green scrubs, a giant Gumby,
who carried her
upstairs from the morgue
to nurse at my leaking breasts, dreaming of cabbage leaves.
Remembers.

I don't even remember this
Jolly Green Giant's, Jamaican name.
His eyes a bowl of mercy,
hands on my daughter' 5 pound corpse,
His rolling Caribbean accents,
the sound of his voice
saying to me "Here. Mommy."
Allan wept when he said that,
wishing he could say that
but he could not.

Maybe I brought her outfit
in the black Donna Karan diaper bag,
A baby shower gift from Allan's colleagues

I forgot how I placed her miniature
arms, right then left,
tiny perfect fingernails,
beautiful dead digits,
Her fingers and toes somehow intact.
Did I flinch over the beauty of her toes?

II.
Did I move one stiff leg,
A little Lincoln log,
into the mercy of the color pink
Shoving a right limb after a left?
Did I remember the matching
pink polka dot spotted socks,
Her white rabbit booties
so that her feet would not get cold
that January day
she left the hospital,
dressed in a body bag?

Maybe I chose the pink fleece
snow suit that I bought with the gift card
from The Children's Place—
A baby gift from Odell, my deputy director,
The only colleague who always made me laugh
before Charlotte died,
I don't laugh much anymore.

III.
I no longer recall
If I left her diaper in place,
or if I changed her, out of habit,
Irrelevant body fluids now
Compared to my two sons diapers
who did not die in childbirth.

IV.
I do not know
If the elastic waistband stretched
around her perfect Cornish waist,
the waist that was almost named Tamson,
Allan's choice.
So little of Charlotte's birth
or death was Allan's choice.

V.
This much I know.
She was dressed or not dressed
when she was cremated.
I remember I wore grief.

One By One They Say

"You lost so much weight."
I am still not hungry.
I forget to eat, emaciated
by the force of ordinary things.
Now, I am bones and motions,
the mechanics of days and demands.
Her ashes serve as evidence that she was almost here.
She stays in my kitchen in a cheap Chinese
pink colored heart, a biscuit tin.

Maybe a year passes and is gone.
I smoke and cry and deteriorate.
I don't rise out of bed, shower,
get dressed for a long time.
Two years of perpetual bathrobes.

I neglect my sons.
That I wake in the morning and brush my teeth,
is more nothing. The daily chores elude me now.
I move more slowly in spite of less weight.
I open the refrigerator, *where is the bread?*
"Did I buy milk, or remember to feed
my sons?"

Tragedy Does That

Tragedy does that: changes the shape of things.
My eyes adopt the color of sorrow,
whether opened or closed.
When spring arrives, pink petunias and pansies
bloom obscene.

My family shatters and never repairs.
The marriage dies.
Her father abandons me and doesn't return.
Nothing remains after Charlotte.
It is one more loss and every loss.
The violence of living consumes me.
I am alone now
in a way more powerful and permanent
than loneliness.

God Doesn't Live at Our House Anymore

I.
My sons are with me when a OB/GYM resident announces
my daughter is dead. Their baby sister.
I look at them.
Alex is five. Jake is seven.
I cannot protect them from this.
Cannot offer a medical reason or even a lie to comfort them.
The boys grow old overnight.
Their father comes and gets them from the hospital.
He tells them. Childhood ends.

II.

My son Jake states
"God doesn't live at our house anymore."
I cannot deny this brutal truth.
I say to him, "There is no God."
He is not even eight years old.

We stop being Jews.
It is no longer relevant, or comforting.
So, we simply cease to believe in anything
We don't go to temple anymore.
When rabbi comes to our house,
the boys refuse to come downstairs,
afraid of the Aramaic
prayers for the dead—a foreign
language rendered instantly familiar
One we will say every January, every August
in Fire Island where her ashes are scattered.

III.
My nanny and Marielos dismantle
her nursery in what was Jake's bedroom,
that he sacrificed willingly for his sister.

Charlotte is all of our sacrifices.
When she dies, he never sleeps in his room,
again, no matter what color we paint it.
No shade or layers cover this magnitude of loss.
Her absence stronger than the presence of my sons.
They are never the same boys,
just as I am never the same mother.
Jake tells me: *"You are 43 years old.*
You have to stop crying."
My grief contained, as if my bathtub, with its vessel of tears, were a
chapel or prison.
There is no longer any difference between the two, at least not for me.

I look in the rear-view mirror at where her car seat should be.
as we drive to little league, the boys fight in the backseat—
hit each other with sharp objects.
I am suddenly repulsed by male emotions.
By the time we reach the baseball field,
I am ignited with rage, flattened by duty.
I wish I could leave them to the cruelty of April
travel to forbidden places, lose my maternal instinct to return.

The Language of Survival

I.
Mutable beggar wings.
I predict the dead will not return
for the unborn butterflies,
lost in a garden of red caterpillars.
My regret, the color of poppies,
portends a decade of complicated grieving—
A smoke alarm bleeds onto a starless night.

II.
My younger dreams travel backwards,
turning into my earlier hopeful self.
They escape at night,
when daylight turns the covers down,
tucking itself into the dark.

Then comes the unwanted, unending pattern of recrimination
of telephones ringing, days discarded to the urgency of survival.

III.
Reading a strong page does not restore the hours,
weeks lost to listening to the echo
of whatever happiness
I still carry in her Cesarian scar.
I reconstruct the images of fireflies resting on Pines Lake.

IV.
Poetry announces my most brutal days.
I pay attention now to the music of words,
the distance between phrases beyond my grasp.
Language leads me back to the five senses,
muted by the immaculate and absolute perfection of letters.
The hieroglyphics of lost, broken things. ()
A skinny day of joy
when I once read the clouds
before the gray mourning obscured my view.

V.
Now there are only corridors of darkness.
The lonely ambition of desire—
A poem I can't escape from.
A stanza shaped like an organ alights
fades out, leaves cobwebs and limbs,
Raindrops scattered on a lyric field.
after opening lines of drought.
Elements that refuse understanding
yet tell us who we are.
The official language of bereavement bears witness.
Makes the invisible
visible to us again.

VI.
See then now—Forty-four false starts,
translated from forgotten notebooks
singed by fire.
I sleep walk along the highway of lost souls
waiting for a new day to open its wings.
I forbid myself from intervening
in other people's mistakes,
their stories a narrative of
The Isle of Skye.

I learn the language of survival,
reside in the darkest house
unforgiving and relentless in its sorrow.

Scavenger Girl

I.

I discard sacred things
that no longer serve me:
My daughter's ashes, grey gravel chasm
churns across the Atlantic Ocean
still manacled to my heart.
I swallow my panic.

Every door locks behind me.

II.

I wander across the crimson mangrove swamps,
searching: for a poem of instruction,
lost keys, years of Monday mornings.
I pray to St. Anthony
to recover prior states of being,
like my daughter Charlotte kicking my stomach the day
before she died.

What I Don't Remember

I
I don't remember talking about people dying
when my friend left me his record collection.
How do you have conversations
about record albums
when everyone around me
injects AIDS medications
between blue toes?

II
It feels brutal to betray my past
by not remembering, yet
I cannot.
No more room for more then the 1,203 eulogies I wrote after overdose,
or AIDS related complications.

III.
Instead,
I remember shaving the legs
of a pregnant woman whom I loved as much as my own handwriting,
engraving the name of our dead daughter
on my stoical British heart.

IV.
I have become a man of sparse words.
At night, a haunting flashback
of her mother's insatiable hands
scouring my bones.
She was my fire, a dormant volcano,
I was an icicle in her dark cave—
that drove a stake through her molten heart.

She is who I remember now,
though I refuse to call her name out loud.
Her name has too many consonants,
Her syllables, infinite.

I need to live in a world of only vowels
which demand nothing of me in return.

V.
I remember her as my former self.
She is the sonogram,
She is the heartbeat,
She is the black and white image
on my old refrigerator in Inwood,
next to the photo of us in Toronto
when we would wonder
about Cornish baby names, Tamsin.
Choosing Charlotte.
Or maybe Charlotte chose us.
I no longer know
what I used to know.

VI.
Charlotte—the January comet
who broke apart my world,
who ate my earth—
as if she and her mother
were wildfire that burned down
every Weeping Willow tree
in the forest of our mutual heart.
My branches rendered kindling.
Now, nothing grows in the wood of my soul,
except a memory of
my English landscape invading her Latina soul.

She reminds me of the Malvinas Islands
That I invaded for a brief interval,
My navy stronger than her teak canoe.
She was a woman of reeds and grass,
woven together in intricate but fragile strips
which unraveled in the merciless Argentine sea.
I landed in her fertile soil, in the essence of her.

When I abandoned her,
I imagined in the distance a white flag wearing
a red heart of her own blood, the one she ripped out—
offered to me like the apple in the Garden of Eden.
I deserted her to grow new ribs,
bones I rebuilt to protect my own fragile heart,
the one I regret not offering to her,when it was still ripe.

Dismantling the Shrine

I.

I take memory as it comes,
I remember her nursery, the mobile
singing dinosaurs—"Good night Moon"
I would have read to her as a bedtime story,
if she had lived.
If only she had lived.

II.

I take memory as it comes,
approach sadness from an acute angle,
Grief—its own Pythagorean Theory:
multiplied exponentially to form a perfect galaxy.
My life is no longer congruent,
not an integer, or a whole number
void of even or odd.,
My sorrow as infinite as π

III.

If I were a circle—
Charlotte would be my radius—
Her death my diameter.
How long the circumference of bereavement?
Is it four beers and a shot of Jameson's?
Or perhaps the volume
a missing space assumes
in the loneliness of my own bedroom.

I hide the evidence in the bottom of my clothes' closet
amongst the size zero skirts.
Work clothes hanging fallow like untilled lands
desperate for harvest.

I haven't worn any of those pencil skirts with flirtatious hems,
since I lost my stomach to Charlotte: my third Cesarean scar.

IV.
If you had warned me
I would become seriously permanently mentally ill
after Charlotte passed away,
that I would return to the Starbucks straw
sliced on a special slant
after twenty-four years of abstinence,
that the faraway were as nearby
as the inside of my mourner's wrist,
Would I even attempt to rise again and dip
my toes into another merciless day?

V.
Prayer, the hours
that open their wings, a fledgling
finding its way blindly back to the nest.
How painful the symbiosis between the dying and those who grieve
them.

VI.
The umbilical cord
Allan cut that I forgot to save—lost to hospital waste.
It becomes hazardous material, Toxic.
Even the most stoical of mothers
smash against the stillborn shore,
flattened by the oppressive
vertical and horizontal days.
Days more horizontal than vertical,
waiting for an explanation some
doctors have yet to discover.
But I have.

VII.
I am evidence of the vortex
of dangerous currents and deadly undertow.
My interior life is a
run-on sentence absent punctuation marks—

a story told by an unreliable narrator,
an afternoon sonnet of despair, disorienting
in its random and unwelcome arrival.

I participate willingly in this ritual of guilt and blame.
The enemy within more powerful
than the infinite danger without—
her death a switchblade shoved in my mourners' dry eye.

VIII.
The symbol of a pink Longchamps suitcase
I packed for the maternity ward
which remained unopened. Gratuitous.
rendered meaningless now that I lost her father under a silver moon.

IX.
I bury the "I."
There is no longer first person singular,
What remains is we, I admire how she and I
become reduced to one syllable of repressed longing.
This is the poetry of Complicated Grieving.
The blinding, unlikely
flash of lightning striking twice
setting fire to everything in its wake,
rendering us dust.

The Prodigal Daughter

If my father were a star
He would splash across the sky
like a burning comet of crimson flames
So angry they shame the stop lights.
He crashes to earth
The cruel chance of lightning
striking twice
killing every tree his rage ignites
His staff, his hail, his brimstone
His curse severing me at the trunk
"You have ruined this family."
I bow down in repentance,
my family's sacrifice
so submissively surrendered,
that nobody notices I have gone,
remembers my name,
the one shame branded me with.
My crime too heinous to
deserve its own noun.